1

Ahmed Iqbal Ullah Race Relations Archive 2004

Published by Ahmed Iqbal Ullah Race Relations Archive and Education Trust, Ground floor, Devonshire House, University Precinct Centre, Oxford Road, Manchester, M13 9PL

The Ahmed Iqbal Ullah Race Relations Archive and Education Trust is grateful for financial support for this project from Manchester City Council, The Progress Trust and The University of Manchester.

Financial assistance and support towards the development and production of this book was provided by the Community Chest.

Edited by Nilufa Khanum, Alaha Sultana, Tanya Miah, Rumana Aktar, Monica Miah, supported by Emma Britain and Ann Hardy.
Designed by Emma Britain.
Transcription by Kay Welby.
Translation by Yasmin Begum.

'Strength of Spirit' is the result of interviews with Bangladeshi women in Manchester that took place in 2003. We wish to thank all the women who have allowed their stories and experiences to be included, especially to the women of Ananna and Krishti. Thanks also go to the teachers at Levenshulme High School for Girls and Burnage High School for Boys who supported this project: particularly Melanie Pettifer and Yasmin Begum. Thanks to all who donated photographs including the Longsight Sylhet Link Group.

Printed by Pelican Press 20 Pollard Street East, Ancoats, Manchester, M40 7ET.
British Library cataloguing in publication data:
A catalogue record for this book is available from the British Library
ISBN 0-9542874-2-8

AHMED IQBAL ULLAH
RACE RELATIONS
ARCHIVE

Ahmed Iqbal Ullah
Education
Trust

Levenshulme
HIGH SCHOOL

MANCHESTER
CITY COUNCIL

THE UNIVERSITY
of MANCHESTER

Strength of Spirit

*The Lives and experiences of Bangladeshi women
from Manchester*

3

Table of Contents

Foreword

The Community History Project was devised by the Ahmed Iqbal Ullah Race Relations Archive. Working in several schools in Manchester, the project set out to support young South Asian people in collecting oral histories within their own ethnic communities.

We believe it is very important that young people know their family and community histories, but the stories of Manchester's minority groups do not form part of the school curriculum. This project was, for most of the young people involved, a first opportunity to really explore their own community history in a formal way – beyond listening to the reminiscences of elders around the dinner table.

Students from different schools have explored various communities:
Oakwood High School - Sikh community in Chorlton and Whalley Range
Levenshulme and Burnage High Schools - Bangladeshi community in Longsight and Levenshulme
Abraham Moss High School - Pakistani community in the Cheetham Hill and Crumpsall areas.

Many of those interviewed are family and friends of the students. The project does not pretend to be a comprehensive survey or representation of the diversity of the South Asian communities in Manchester. Through the project students have developed skills in research, interviewing, video, writing and editing, while focused on history that engaged and affirmed their identity as Mancunians with a South Asian heritage.

This book has been produced by Bangladeshi young women from Levenshulme High School who interviewed women in their own community. Other interviews were conducted by students from Burnage High School. From the findings, the young women wanted to document 'Herstory': to acknowledge the achievements of Bangladeshi women and recognise the mental, emotional and physical effects of their migration and settlement to Manchester.

The women have shared their experiences of life in Bangladesh with family and friends, and of moving to England. For each of them, a life in England meant a social context of a different language and culture. A feeling of isolation was common as it was often hard to feel part of the wider community. The students note that:

"Through interviews conducted with Bangladeshi women, we have documented some of their views and feelings about family life, society,education, work, the War of Independence, being a woman, the motherland and England. We hope to achieve some recognition for these women who have spent most of their lives providing for their families, community and family businesses. There is more to Bangladeshi women than some people think.Their accounts have been very educational and inspiring".

In contrast to stereotyped views of 'the Asian woman', the personal stories contained in this book reveal much diversity of experience, ideas and opinions. If the local histories of minority communities in Manchester are infrequently told, those of minority women are further marginalised. The young women of Levenshulme High School have, in this book, made a magnificent contribution to revealing the hidden 'herstory' of Bangladeshi women in Manchester.

Jacqueline Ould, Ann Hardy and Emma Britain
Ahmed Iqbal Ullah Education Trust.

Introduction: From Bangladesh to Manchester

By Nilufa Khanum and Alaha Sultana, Levenshulme High School

Bangladesh won its Independence in 1971, but long before that it was a country with its own language, history, culture and tradition. Throughout the history of Bengal, music, literature, painting, medicine, science and agriculture were greatly developed. As early as the Gupta era (320-467AD), Bengali merchant ships carried a thriving trade to different countries. At the beginning of the 13th century, Islam was introduced by armies from Afghanistan. By 1500, the Mughal Empire had reached Northern India.

In the 1700s, India became part of the British Empire, coveted for its wealth and trade. The British ruled for 200 years until 1947, when India gained independence and the state of Pakistan was founded. The area of modern Bangladesh was incorporated into the new state as East Pakistan. A bloody War of Independence was fought, under the leadership of Sheikh Mojibur Rahman. The right to speak and learn in Bengali was not recognised by the Pakistan government and this was a very important part of the struggle for independence. Eventually, in 1971, Bangladesh gained its national independence.

Bangladesh is one of the world's most densely populated countries. It has four major religions: Islam, Christianity, Buddhism and Hinduism, with about 85 percent of the people being Muslims. Dhaka is the capital. It was founded in 1608AD by the Mughal Emperors and is known as the 'City of Mosques.'

Bangladesh has some of the world's most fertile agricultural land and because the temperatures are high crops can be grown all year round. The main crops grown are rice, jute, sugar cane and tea, which are exported. Bangladesh is also a major exporter of manufactured clothes.

Towards the end of the 18th Century, many farmers in British India lost their land. Poverty drove many Sylheti men to leave home to work abroad on British ships in order to earn a living. These sailors were called Lascars and they became the first Sylheti settlers in Britain. Men from India and other Commonwealth countries fought in the battles of both World Wars. Soon after the Second World War, Britain suffered a shortage of labour. The government invited people from Commonwealth countries to come and work in the UK and so more of the Bangladeshi population started to arrive in Britain.

Some Bangladeshi settlers moved North to jobs in the textile industry. Most of the men were single and originally wanted to earn enough money to go back to Bangladesh. Others came to Britain to complete their studies. Bangladeshi people in Manchester have worked hard to build community organisations. The Greater Manchester Bangladeshi Association (GMBA), the Bangladeshi Women's Project (Ananna, meaning unique) and Krishti (the Bangladeshi Women's Cultural Group) are just some of the organisations that aim to help and represent the views of the Bangladeshi population in Manchester. Many of Manchester's "Indian" restaurants are in fact owned and staffed by Bangladeshis.

With this book we want to recognise the achievements of the women in our community and show that we are grateful for the support they provide us.

A Personal Memory of Bangladesh

Banugaz is an extremely beautiful village. In front of my village is a fast flowing river, which leads into the forest behind my house. There are three large 'fuqurs' ponds in front of my house that are filled with so many different types of fish. Sometimes my sisters, brothers and I would see kingfishers making their nests near these ponds. Once I even saw a kingfisher laying her eggs! "We would often see the kingfishers catching fish for their children.

The forest was a home to so many different kinds of animals - they include Royal Bengal tigers, cheetahs, wolves, deer, monkeys, and so many different types of snakes and wild chickens. I would often be dazzled by the different arrays of colours that the wild chickens were. Then of course, we also had the ordinary animals such as rabbits, foxes, hedgehogs, pigs and ducks.

The forest was so large that it went on to connect to India's forests. There were also so many types of tropical birds that would live in the forest during the spring and summer. There were trees in our village that were over 200 years old. They were gigantic! My dad made a swing that hung down one of the branches of one of these old trees. I used to have endless hours of fun just swinging.

We could not leave anything outside of the house because the monkeys would steal them. The monkeys would come twice a year. There were literally thousands of them! They would come when the fruit in the forest was ripe. There were so many monkeys in the trees that you couldn't see the leaves on the trees. The villagers had to keep dogs to scare the monkeys away because they would destroy everything that was growing in the fields and the vegetable patches. My sisters and I would be too scared to go out because once a monkey chased us when we went to my auntie's house.

In the night all the doors were kept locked and everyone had to stay in. No-one was allowed out because the tigers would come roaming around the houses. They would kill the cows and sheep and drag them back into the forest to eat it. Once or twice they even killed our dogs.

In my spare time I would often go swimming in the ponds and walk around the forests with my dad or uncle. I would never go alone because I was too scared. I would pick flowers and beetle nuts. I would also pick fruit from the trees and take them home with me to eat. My brothers and sisters and I would get bamboo and my dad would carve it into toys for us to play with.

Chapter One

Arrival

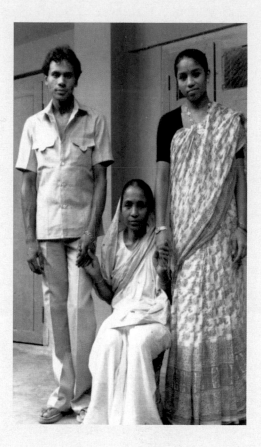

Expectations of Manchester

"It was nothing like I'd dreamt of. Naturally, everybody dreams of a city before going into that city, and I always thought, "Oh England, rich like America." I went to Australia and America before I came to England, so I found it actually ... especially Manchester – at that time in the 80s it was less developed."

I came with my husband, thinking I would get an easy life here, and when I arrived, it was the way I expected it to be.

I had been told about England, before actually moving, by family and friends. I expected England to be better in many ways, such as school and healthwise. I wanted a better life for my family. I guess in some way I got what I wanted from coming to England, which is a better life for my family. I feel I had more freedom here because I have to work to earn a living.

I came to England five years after my daughter was born in 1986. I brought with me a 'qu'ran shorif', a 'wozifa', and clothes for me and my children. I thought that England would be a beautiful place. I heard stories that England had no fields and that it was all concrete. I thought that everyone would have mansions and lots of luxuries. I thought that poverty was not even an issue in Britain.

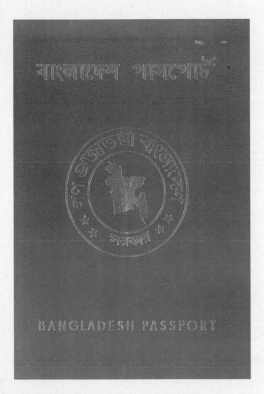

I thought it would be more a dream, Manchester, but no! When the plane was landing from New York to London, London to Manchester. I felt so hopeless that it's not a big city, I mean I could not see many big buildings, maybe the plane did not come through the big buildings. So I saw cows grazing, and my plane landed in the cows grazing!

Reasons for Coming to Manchester

We came to England from Chittagong in 1999 because my husband came to study. It was hard to get used to Manchester but mixing with other people is easy and I have found English people to be very kind. I miss my parents and siblings, but although I would like to return to Bangladesh my home is here now.

I was born in Manchester and went to Bangladesh. We came back from Bangladesh when I was about six. The reason we came back is that it was shortly after the Independence War, and my parents felt that we needed an education, and perhaps it was actually better that we came back to the UK, back to England.

Being in Manchester

After I arrived in England, I attended the Education Centre in Manchester, where I did not have to wear a uniform. Everyone was very nice, kind and helpful, and no-one said anything to me. I knew a bit of English before I arrived here, but I was not fluent. I had a lot of English and Pakistani friends, and had support from my husband, but still I found it very hard to fit in.

I would often feel frustrated, as everything I seemed to do was hard work. Although I was a housewife in Bangladesh and I didn't have a washing machine or dishwasher, we had servants that would do the washing for me. Here you had to do everything alone and it was so much hard work.

The houses in England were smaller than the houses in Bangladesh. I came at a time when everything was available to me. When shopping before, I found it hard to purchase halal food, but now it is easier as the community is more mixed than before.

As a six year-old, I was very shocked by the dress of the women. Miniskirts were in fashion; women were exposing their legs, so for me it was very shocking. I remember sitting on the plane, and we came by British Airways, because at that point Bangladesh didn't have its own airline and British Airways were flying planes from Dhakar to London. The air hostesses were all English, and they were obviously wearing skirts and tights. I'd never seen tights before, so every time an air hostess went past, I kept stroking her leg to feel her tights. And she kept looking at me and smiling, and I think she must have been used to it, because I think a lot of children probably stroked her legs to feel this material on her!

I sometimes found it hard to communicate with others, but when I came here I started to study English and I took lessons for factory work. As time went on I found myself making more friends. I did find it hard to fit in at first but then found people like myself.

I was the first person to settle in Manchester in my family, but we have relatives in London. I found it hard to get used to the place and area because the surroundings were different to me at first. The easiest thing in England to me was to mix with others, because it's a multicultural area. I found it easy to fit in with my community and did not receive any racist remarks, nor did I feel unwanted.

I was a bit shocked because it was very cold.

Chapter Two

Family

Our Childhood

We had a wonderful, wonderful time, because my mum and dad were important government people. We had a high status in the country - hospitals, office cars, private cars, - we had all the best facilities. I've also had all the privileges from the army - I had a scholarship from the national army, a special scholarship, plus I was a good student and I got a scholarship from the government.

Our parents gave us the opportunity to pursue our education, and also we were allowed to speak our mind. We used to talk about everything in our family.

Our family was quite modern and they taught us how to cope with the modern world. We had uncles and aunties going abroad, living abroad, and they used to come back and teach us – "In England they do it like this, America they do it like this."

My dad was a British navy officer when he started his career, but then he became an army officer. My mum has recently retired. She was a Senior Section officer in the Ministry of Bangladesh Establishment Department and a senior officer of women's welfare. She served all her life in the ministry, and she wanted her children to join the government services, but we didn't. So she's angry with me that I haven't followed in her footsteps.

My father, he really worried about us. If we went somewhere and didn't come back or were 5 minutes late, my father would be at the door, waiting. He was quite liberal , but he was very strict as well - we couldn't go out, not even school trips or college trips. I didn't go to the cinema until I was in the second year of medical school when I was 19!

My family mean the world to me. My mum is extremely supportive in everything that I do. I am extremely grateful to her for that and deep down I love her dearly and know that she is truly a mum in a million! She brought up six children single handedly after my dad left and I know that this would have been extremely hard for her. I really hope that I make my mother proud of me and I achieve her expectations of me because at the end of the day that's all that matters to me.

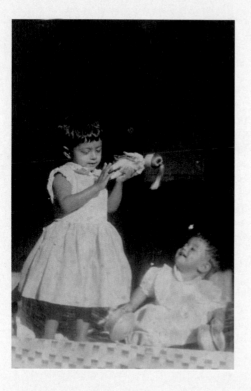

In my view family is very important - at the end of the day I have someone to turn to. They guide me, help me when I am in need, and respect me for who I am and the decisions I make. Your family brings you happiness. They are always there for you. I love my family a lot, without them I would not be where I am.

Our Children

I have two children. One is nearly fifteen and the other is fourteen. I wish them success. I want them to achieve their goals in life. I might be imagining too much, but I'd like them to achieve; study hard; do a good job. Good life. Progress - not the life I'm going through now.

I think that the way I was brought up and the way I am bringing up my children are completely different. We were brought up in two different societies and cultures. Whereas I went picking flowers and fishing, my children go out with their friends or just sit and watch TV. They have much more freedom than I did. I was chaperoned everywhere I went.

In a way I feel sorry for them. They haven't seen half the things I have seen. They find it hard to believe that tigers and snakes roaming around my house in Bangladesh was nothing unusual. They are scared of chickens and ducks! They haven't got a river or forest at the back of their house. They can't pick a mango from a tree whenever they want. They have to go to the supermarket and buy one.

I do sometimes think about going back to Bangladesh permanently. However, I don't think my children want to go back with me, and I really don't want to go alone to live in Bangladesh.

My achievement is my children, They are all educated and they all
have a degree - of that I'm quite pleased.

I have three children - three girls. I think it's very difficult bringing up children and all parents struggle to make the right decisions for their children. In this community it's even harder. Being a Bangladeshi or any ethnic minority and living in a British society is very difficult because you want your children to have the values of your culture and your religion, and at the same time they live in a society and a culture that's very different from their home culture.

As a parent, you have to do a lot of balancing and that is difficult at times. Then you have the added pressure of having to work and having to fit in other things around bringing children up.

I would say that bringing children up means you have to communicate with your children so they understand if you're saying no, why you are saying no and what the cultural context is that you're saying no for. It is hard work because you constantly have to be talking to your children so that they understand the decisions that you've made.

I wish for them to have a contented life, a life that they're happy with. I want them to have health, and I want them to feel that they've led a successful or fulfilling life, and that's enough for me really.

Chapter Three

Education

Education in Bangladesh

After breakfast I would go swimming in the pond. I would have a few snacks and then set off for school at ten o'clock. It was a thirty-minute walk to school and school would start at 10.30 a.m. so by the time we arrived, school was about to begin.

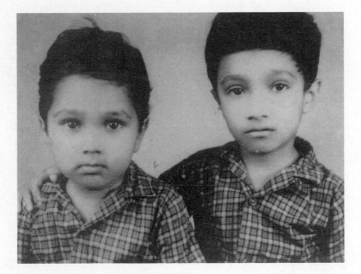

My primary school was mixed. At school we would learn Bangla, Maths, History, Science and about Islam. We never had any practical lessons because we did not have equipment to do practicals with - it was all written work.

I was educated in Bangladesh until I graduated. I actually received higher education than my brothers. I was taught Maths MBA, and did two semesters in Business Administration. I haven't received any education in England, but I want to do higher studies here.

The teacher had a cane and if we were naughty he would hit us on our hand. I was not very good at Maths, and once or twice I did get hit. We would have a thirty-minute break for lunch. There was no canteen so we would have to go to the shops in order to buy our lunch. After eating we would play hide and seek, skip and hopscotch. Then the caretaker would ring a bell and we would run back to class. School would end at 3.30 p.m.

In Bangladesh, I only got a home education, until I was aged Sixteen/ Seventeen. A private tutor used to come and teach us. I didn't go to school or college but I've been to college here in England.

It was my father who inspired me to become a doctor. My father always wanted all his daughters to be educated before they got married, so if anything bad happened in their life they could maintain themselves. He felt strongly that girls should be educated.

I was educated in Bangladesh up to college. I received the same amount of education in my family as the men did.

English Schools

We did wear a uniform but the uniform was not very culturally sensitive because anybody who wanted to cover their legs had to wear trousers. So we had to have this standard uniform which was a jumper or a cardigan with a blouse underneath, and a skirt. If you wanted to cover your legs you had to wear trousers under your skirt, so we'd have all these Asian girls wearing trousers plus a skirt on top. It's only now that it's become fashionable to wear a skirt on top of trousers, but in those days it was very embarrassing – you looked horrible in your school uniform.

I think there's more multicultural reinforcement now within schools. It might be a way to combat the differences. There are so many differences when there are lots of numbers in a different group. It creates some kind of tension between students in school, and they've got to educate people about it.

They didn't cater for the different religious foods, like halal and kosher, it was just school meals. Even for non-meat eaters - I don't think they even had a vegetarian dish for non-meat eaters. There were also problems with Hijab and Sikhs and their turbans. Hijab wasn't allowed; in PE all the girls had to wear knickers and a white vest and the boys had to wear blue shorts and a white vest. Nowadays Muslim girls can wear leggings or tights.

I think when we went to school, we went to school to learn the alphabet, do the maths. Nothing in school was culturally orientated; school was just about learning, educating, reading and writing.

I went to university but it was a very short course! I never actually finished the course because the university was situated away from my house and I had to live there five days of the week. I think my parents decided it was time for me to get married, and soon afterwards I did. But I'm sure that if I had gone to the university in Manchester, I would have finished my course. I think the fact that I had to live away from home that was a problem. It's threatening to mothers and fathers.

I don't think I experienced any racism when I was at college. When I came to this country from Bangladesh it was in the Seventies. There were a lot of skinheads around, and 'Paki-bashing' was very fashionable, it was the done thing. So if you went out and saw skinheads and you were Black or Asian then you were usually afraid.

I do remember running home from school on a number of occasions trying to avoid older boys. I remember one lunchtime having to come home for lunch, and being stopped by a gang of boys who, thinking about it now, were about twelve or thirteen. All they were doing was messing about really, but for a six-year-old, or a seven year-old, it was really terrifying, being very scared and hoping somebody would come so that you could go home safely.

Comparisons

I did study in Bangladesh, and also I went abroad. I went to Australia – I did demographic coursework there for a Masters degree. And also I did Public Administration and Sociology in America.

I went to school very briefly in Bangladesh, and I remember going to a school which had a very old teacher who used to fall asleep! So all the children used to leave the class and go running around eating berries from the tree, and then they used to quickly run back when they thought he was waking up! I didn't go to school for long, it was only for a few weeks, but I remember that. In England I went to infant school because I was six years' old – my first memory is falling off the climbing frame on my first day at school, and being too embarrassed and too scared to tell the teacher that I'd fallen off!

I found the education in Bangladesh very hard – the education in England was a lot easier.

Importance of school

I think education is important for women to establish themselves in this society. My mum was educated in Bangladesh until the age of 16. She got married at the age of 18. She has many hopes and dreams for her children, wanting us to have the further education she did not have so if any problems occur in the future we are financially stable.

My studies help me to be positive, because Bangladesh was a very competitive country at that time. Women were nowhere. They could not be given the scholarships and did not have a high status, because there was more male supremacy at that time. But going into different countries helped and gave me a higher education, and also education from the Western perspective. I could represent Bangladesh and people used to call me an ambassador. I also got a higher degree scholarship from America, so my picture came out in the newspaper there.

I wish to go to university after college to continue my studies in Engineering so I can become an engineer in the future. There are many things I wish to do in life. I hope to be sucessful and no matter how many times I fall down I will pick myself back up again. I am happy that my parents are supporting me.

I have been brought up in a family where it was never a question as to whether I should go on to further education after my GCSEs or not. I have high hopes for my future, however I know that it won't be handed to me on a plate. I am willing to put in that hard work, commitment and dedication into my studies to achieve my goals. I know how important education is and that it is the key to success.

I think one of my proudest moments has to be when my daughter was offered a place at Oxford University. She's studying at Wadham College now, and reading English literature and French, so I'm very proud of her. For our family it's a first! Out of my family, my husband's family, my mother's family, no-one has ever been to Oxford University. So for somebody from my background and from my family to go to Oxford University is something to be very proud of. I think increasingly I'm pleased when I hear about other Bangladeshis going to Oxford. It shows that the Bangladeshi community is achieving.

Chapter Four

Marriage

I got married at the age of seventeen, a month before I was eighteen. I'd just about finished my GCSEs then. My parents really didn't want to agree at that time because I was quite young, but I was the eldest daughter. It was the beginning of the 80s, late 1970s; girls were getting married at seventeen, eighteen. Before that, our parents got married a lot, lot younger. So it went with the trend. Nowadays the girls are married after a degree and after a secure job, which is in the mid-20s, if not, early 30s. If you'd heard that 20 years ago, it would have been an outrage.

It was done traditionally at the mosque, then we had it at the registry in town, and we did the traditional mendhi. We had a little party - followed by the marriage, over the period of a weekend.

I had an arranged marriage, and I don't know what to say. I met my husband at the airport - he came with my cousin and my cousin's brother, and we saw each other and liked each other. I came here for seven days and he said to my brother, "Tell your sister to stay and not to go back!". My family also liked him, and that's how we got married.

It was an arranged marriage, but we were given the opportunity to meet, and my father said if I didn't like him, I didn't have to marry him. But when we met, we liked each other. It was interesting. It doesn't feel interesting any more though!

Issues with arranged marriages

At one point, the girl didn't have a choice. I think when our aunties and mothers got married, their parents found a boy, and this was who you got married to, end of story. They grew up with that culture and they believed that parents know what's best, the parents love the child, they won't do anything to hurt the child, they'll always want the best for their daughter.

I don't support forced marriage, but I support arranged marriage if it is done properly. Keeping the interest of the girl and the boy. Sometimes a lot of arranged marriages are carried out to benefit the relatives or somebody else. I don't agree with that. And I think that girls and boys should be at a proper age to decide for themselves as well, and their opinion should be counted.

They don't want their daughters to struggle because of the marriage break-ups. They make sure that their daughters all become educated, and even after education where they've got a job, they're earning x thousands of pounds, in order that they can stand on their own two feet.

But how independent do they become? Because again, when they're looking for their son, a daughter for their son, they want a traditional, typical Bengali, and yet they educate their sisters to the extreme, so it's hard to find a husband for her. And obviously, if she is educated or employed, she's not going to be a typical housewife.

One thing that does exist is independence. I don't think women had much independence, but now, you're yourself, you are who you are. You're not defined by your husband or your dad, but we grew up in that 'cloudy' time. Nobody before us had this modern sense of arranged marriages, an introductory marriage, where two people are introduced.

Mixed marriages

I personally am not in favour of mixed marriages, because I feel that it's very difficult for the next generation. OK, husband and wife are from a mixed background, but for the children it's hard for them to establish their identity – are they white? Are they black? Are they Muslim? Are they Christian? Where do they fit in? And I think for that reason it's very difficult.

I think that the reality is that our community, our society isn't really ready for mixed marriages. I think not only do the children have a difficult time, I think also the husband and wife have a very difficult time, because families may not be accepting of that kind of arrangement. Life is hard enough as it is, and we don't need to add more complications to that.

To be honest, I think to marry your own kind is the choice of mine, but I'm not against it either. If anything, if two persons get together, with love and sincerity, I can't see anything wrong with the mixed marriage. That's my personal opinion. My eldest daughter married an English man, a Yorkshire man; he's quite decent and very highly educated. First we had a little shock, but we accepted it. They've been married the last eighteen years. I often see the girls having mixed marriages nowadays, and this is because the place people are growing up in is mixed. To marry someone decent I don't think is bad at all.

I personally think that it is very difficult, and I would not like my children to have a mixed marriage. But they might think differently when they're growing up and making those decisions. I believe that my children will want to marry a Bangladeshi, and more importantly for that person to be a Muslim.

Chapter Five

Memories of the War

When the Liberation war began in 1971 I was in Bangladesh. I remember standing by the pond early in the morning. I saw a group of soldiers marching towards my home. More people started to see what was going on. The soldiers raided everyone's houses. They beat up the men. When everyone realised what was happening, the women all went by boat to the next village.

Towards the east of my house was a Hindu village. The soldiers burnt all the houses there. All the Hindu men and women came to hide in the Muslim people's houses. They went on to the next village after that and did the same thing. They did this to most of Bangladesh. I remember hearing about a village where the soldiers lined up all the Muslim and Hindu old men, women and young children and blindfolded them. They then shot them one by one. The young men and women in the village were taken away to camps.

Whoever the soldiers found they would kill - no one was shown mercy. The soldiers came to my in-laws' house. When they came we had to dig bunkers between bamboo trees and hide.

The soldiers never came to my parents' village because it was near the forest, and they were scared that the Bengali Freedom Fighters would hide there, ready to attack them. I had to have an identification pass that would allow me to travel to my parents' home. There were soldiers in the streets that you would have to show it to. If you did not have it they would kill you.

Thousands and thousands of people were given asylum in India. Without India it would have been an even harder struggle for Bangladesh to gain its freedom.

They were targeting particular groups – I remember my dad being in the target group because he was a British citizen. Anybody who was from abroad and was educated was a target. I remember on one occasion he had been picked up by the army – the camp was about ten miles from where we lived, and at that time my dad was building a house. He was stopped by the 'border patrol' as you would call it, and was made to show his identity card.

Then he was taken into the camp, and my dad told us that he thought they would kill him then. Because he could speak Urdu, he could speak to the guards. And the guards would say, "Oh, I've got a cousin who lives in Manchester, do you know him?" And my dad said, "Yes yes, I know him and I work with him." So the guard said, "Have you got any jumpers from England?" And my dad said, "yes I have - Let me go home and I'll bring it back for you," and the guard let him go on that pretext! It was a narrow escape for him!

My mum lost members of her family during the independence. She had a cousin who was an army surgeon and his son was a medical student at the time. The army came and picked them both up and they never came back. We have heard that they were actually killed together, but their bodies have never been found and they've never returned. We've got direct experience of the independence struggle. And we had to leave our home for about six months, and at that time I had a younger brother who died because we couldn't afford the medical treatment that he required at the time.

My family was in Bangladesh at the time of Independence and so was I. I was quite young, probably about five at the time, and I do remember aspects of independence. I do remember having to leave our house in the middle of the night because the Pakistani army were coming towards Sylhet, and everybody was leaving their home and going towards more backward areas in terms of hills and so on, where it would be more difficult to find people.

The flag of Bangladesh is a green background with a red circle. The green represents the land that we fought for and the red stands for how many people died in the war - their blood.

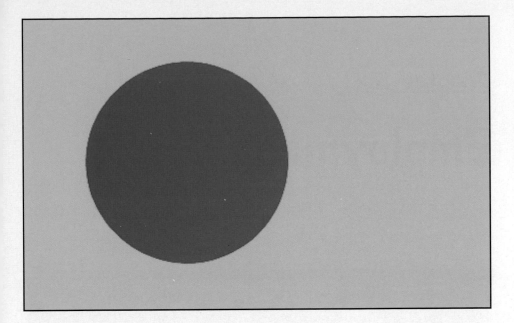

Chapter Six

Employment

In Bangladesh, I come from quite a good family, I'm very proud of that, and I had been taught a lot of good things, good values, good manners, and I have a lot of qualifications from Bangladesh, a Masters and Honours degree from Bangladesh University. And I did a lot of jobs in Bangladesh, while studying and after study. So I had a high salary and a lot of a respect. Here, I feel that job-wise I had to struggle a lot because the societies are completely different jobwise.

I didn't have a job in Bangladesh, although when I arrived in this country I first worked at a factory, but then became a Bengali teacher. It was easy for me to find a job because I was introduced to a lady who also worked there. When I worked at the factory I got paid equally to the men.

When I came here I was told that whatever qualifications and job experience I had, it was our experience that counted – our way of working. So I had to really research into it – what did they mean by 'ours'? So slowly I had to cope by doing voluntary work, and working in the community a bit. I already knew that I had to speak English, so that was not hard for me.

I started as a primary school teacher, as a voluntary teacher for my college professor. She was an American Christian and took us to the slum areas in Dhaka, the capital city of Bangladesh, and told us we had to teach English in this school. It was very shocking – I was crying for two or three days; but my dad said "No no, this will help you, this will be a good thing for your future." I didn't enjoy it because it was a slum area – I didn't like the poverty, going into poverty, and telling them that "I've come to teach you." I was sad and I was jealous and I was proud of myself, you know, "I'm a rich girl and why should I go there to the slum area?" but I learnt so much from that teaching, and the students loved me also.

From there, I have looked and thought about the society we live in, and how human relationships are, and my dad told me, "Now you must go for an English degree, BA Honours in English." And I said,"No no, I want to be a sociologist," and he said, "What for?" So I took the examination - he did not like it, because then it was a modern science, a modern subject. So I did that, and then I got a scholarship from my university. Everywhere, I was getting special attention. That was during the wartime and my dad was killed, so after that incident the teacher and society gave me a very privileged position.

Now I'm a sociologist and during the sociology degree I was offered a very good scholarship in Australia to do research work. I did that, and then I became a demographer, which means studying about population. From there, I came back to Bangladesh – I was doing a beautiful job, and then I got an offer to study a post-graduate degree in America. From there, I came back and then I came to England to visit my family, and here I am! So I've done a lot of study, a lot of work, and now presently I'm doing teaching, because I always told my mum, and mum always told me that, "What is education for? Education is to give away to others – the resources, the knowledge!

জায়গার নয়জন কবি স্বরচিত কবিতা পাঠ করেন। তারা হলেন - সুলতানা নাসরিন, মোঃ আহসান উল্লাহ, ইলিয়াস উদ্দিন, সুলতানা সাদিক রোজী, ম আ মোশতাক, গণি চৌধুরী, আয়েশা সিদ্দিকা, তোসাদ্দুক হোসেন ও তাবেদার রসুল। বাংলাদেশ থেকে আগত জনপ্রিয় বাউল শিল্পী আব্দুল কুদ্দুস বয়াতীর গান সমাগত দর্শক-শ্রোতাদের মাতিয়ে রাখে। ইয়াসমীন আলীর উপস্থাপনায় বাচ্চাদের নাচ ও পোষাক প্রদর্শনী অনুষ্ঠিত হয়। এতে অংশ নেন ফারহানা, পিংকি, বিভা, শাকিলা, সুমি, শেলী, শিরিন প্রমুখ। তোসাদ্দুক হোসেন বাহারের সহযোগিতায় বিশিষ্ট নাট্যকার হুমায়ুন আহমেদের 'স্বপ্ন-বিলাস' মঞ্চস্থ হয়। এতে অভিনয় করেন লিসা ও অপু চৌধুরী। এছাড়াও অনুষ্ঠানে যাদু ও র্যাফেল ড্র অনুষ্ঠিত হয়। অনুষ্ঠানের শেষে উপস্থিত সবাইকে আপ্যায়ন করা হয়।

বাংলা নববর্ষ উপলক্ষে ম্যানচেস্টার বাংলা নববর্ষ উদযাপন পরিষদের উদ্যোগে গত ১৬ই এপ্রিল ম্যানচেস্টার গ্রামার স্কুল হলে এক মনোজ্ঞ কবিতা পাঠ, পোষাক প্রদর্শনী, নাটক ও সঙ্গীতানুষ্ঠানের আয়োজন করা হয়। অনুষ্ঠানে শুভেচ্ছা বক্তব্য রাখেন সলফোর্ড লিংক প্রজেক্টের চেয়ারম্যান ডাঃ জরজিস রহমান, ম্যানচেস্টারের বিশিষ্ট সমাজসেবী কবির আহমদ জেপি ও বাংলাদেশ দূতাবাস ম্যানচেস্টারের সহকারী হাইকমিশনার এসরাজুল আলম। কবি তাবেদার রসুলের উপস্থাপনায় বিভিন্ন

61

I wanted to have a part-time job, and I more or less have had a part time jobs throughout my life, and then at a later stage, two or three years later, I had my first child. Because I was capable of doing some sort of job, it helped within the family. Nowadays, it needs at least two wages to come into the home, to maintain a family and live comfortably. I did secretarial jobs - helping people at work, administration, development work, so it wasn't too bad.

My very first job was at the age of eighteen, after I got married. I had a gap year between college and university and I was looking for something to do, so I decided to work for the Manpower Service commission, which I suppose is like Modern Apprenticeships now or Youth Training Scheme, something like that. It actually paid very little, so I worked 25 hours in a place called Hyde as a community development worker, and I was paid around £54 for that. It was my first experience of working with the Bangladeshi community, and it was interesting. I think it gave me a lot of insight and gave me some indication that what I wanted to do, whatever job I was working in later, would be around people and helping people to do things.

My husband had his own business: he had three branches of a pharmacy for twenty-one years successfully. When he started his business in 1973 it was only a small corner pharmacy! He had a very good relationship with the community and people used to admire him, and we did work with him as well, sometimes the children in the school holidays and I used to work as a shop assistant. Then my husband retired in '94, which was voluntary. He sold the pharmacy, helped all of the staff to get jobs, he loved them.

The first month I was looking for a job, and nobody was helping me, not even my husband, so I really had to go from door to door visiting different offices. And once I went to ask about the council housing system in this country, because I didn't know much about the housing, and I went into an office that I thought was the housing office, but it was the citizen's advice bureau. And the lady I was talking to was so impressed that I was speaking in an American accent, and she really took it as a special situation. She helped me – she said, "Would you be our volunteer?" I got the voluntary work and it was for a month. And right after that I got an offer of a job in the social services department in Manchester City Council.

I volunteer at the Bangladesh Organisation. I'm a member there, and I run the Woman's Bangladeshi Side, since I was in Manchester anyway. And I do things for Oxfam, charitable shops I support. I go there to give them some articles and I do a little shopping there as well, the principle of which is very good.

I helped my husband out with his business at first, and when the business took off I had nothing much to do. I did the book-keeping mainly, and I'd sit in the counter because we had a takeaway to start off with. So I'd take the telephone orders at the counter and things like that. Because I truly believe in family life, and I believe my status was through his status. I didn't believe in having my own identity and my own status, or being a lawyer or a teacher. If I wanted that, I probably would have pursued it and pursued my degree course when I started it, but I left it. We never had anything that we needed, so by that time we already had a child as well. So it really was for financial reasons that I went back to work.

It took a lot of knocks and blows for me to realise what life was about. I took the easy route, I told my mum I thought I was going to be a housewife and I was going to get a business and I'd be well-off, and things like that! We bought our house within eight months of getting married, but the mortgage was a headache.

You can't survive with a mortgage and all that. At the beginning I started renting my rooms out upstairs and we stayed downstairs - we had one room as a back room, the front room was the lounge and we had a kitchen. Upstairs we had our students, and when my daughter was born after the first year, I decided I didn't want any more tenants. So I ended up giving her to my mum and a childminder, and then I actually went out to work. I needed the space - and the tenants were getting on my nerves!

I work for the NHS in Bradford. I've worked in the NHS for ten years and I'm a Head of Service, which basically means I'm an assistant director of services. The area that I'm actually working in is around policy, so my job is to make sure that my organisation has the right policies in place for equality and diversity, and making sure that everybody is included in our services regardless of their age, background, sexuality, gender, all those areas, and making sure that we provide good service to everyone.

Also , I help service managers to look at their services, identify the problems within their service, and try and help them to put it right as well. I also look at developing partnerships with external agencies - working with education, employment services, voluntary organisations, and leisure and housing to make sure that the people who we serve get services outside the health service as well.

I don't think I have actually faced any prejudice within the workplace – if I had, I wouldn't be able to get to the position I have done in a relatively short time. I think a lot of it is about the person who you are, and what kind of messages you give out as well, and I personally have never experienced any racism or prejudice. I have seen colleagues who've been either Black or Asian experience racism and discrimination within the workplace.

The NHS does have a history around discrimination - if you look at the doctors in the Fifties and Sixties after the NHS was set up, a lot of doctors came from the Indian subcontinent and we had a lot of nurses who came from the Caribbean islands. Neither of those groups of professionals have really moved into management, compared to the white doctors or white nurses. Black nurses are not really in high positions, and if you look at black doctors or Asian doctors there are not many as consultants, so there is a discrimination factor there.

Chapter Seven

Culture, Religion and Community

The Importance of Culture and Religion

We only picked up our culture and our religion, our tradition, whatever you want to call it, because our parents taught us in this country. They brought a lot of the value back from Bangladesh with them. Obviously they came over to England very young, but they'd been brought up surrounded by large families, a lot of responsibilities at a very young age, and we picked that up from our parents. And we took it in as part of our daily life. Now, our own daughters, they don't do a quarter of the jobs we did at the age of fifteen!

If you understand your culture, if you respect your own culture you can also respect somebody else's, but if you don't know what your culture's about or you don't follow it, then you think "Oh, come on, ...what is it? It's only this, it's only that, "

No religion will teach hatred against another person's religion. Even the prophets, they went into a non-Muslim house and respected them and ate with them like I said, so if a prophet can do that, why can't you as a human being?

It should be there within the family. At the end of the day I teach my children "do not be ignorant, don't ever believe hype about your own religion, respect other people's religion, and yet keep on with your religion and tradition." As long as it doesn't harm a child, let them be aware of other religions, traditions, colour, creed, and they'll become good citizens of the country. There's too much hatred and bitterness and people misunderstanding each other and problems are occurring. People can't live in peace because they're being too possessive about their own thing, when they don't even know their own religion.

I'm a Muslim by birth. I've so much Islamic knowledge from home, I don't need to be re-educated. I know what Islam is, and I know what Islam isn't. I'm not restricted in Islamic ways, but I believe that religion comes from my heart, and I do my best.

If somebody tells me to go to a church, I don't mind, I'll just go and see what is practised there, and I can compare with my own religion. I have a very good friend who is a Hindu - she brought me to the Hujja Hindu festival. And if I was a strict Muslim I shouldn't be touching the food even, but I don't mind because we have been brought up in all kinds of atmospheres. I've seen Christians in my own country, how they've been and what they go through. I have mixed with Buddhists during my studies. So now I'm multi-religious, multicultural person who happens to be a Muslim.

I believe that if I want to do my religion in this country, nobody can stop me. But there was a problem before, when I came in the 80s, there was not much halal food in Manchester. This has progressed through our people coming more, other Muslim people coming. So I like that, and also the cultural things like saris, dresses and Islamic books and things, and videos - these things have progressed much more in a positive way for us.

The impact of culture and religion

It might sound kind of like we were very antisocial, but it wasn't. I think our parents were trying to protect us, because they thought we couldn't be safe out there, nothing else.

We knew that our friends went to discos and pubs, and we thought, "it's not in our religion, we don't do that, " and that's the end of it. We never ever thought twice about it. Our parents took us to a cinema, and there was only one or two in Manchester, we used to watch a film, and we looked forward to that. That was once in a blue moon. Or if family members came with their daughters.

We were stuck within four walls. At the time we were growing up, we couldn't share our ideas, the part that we were Asian and we were allowed to do this or not allowed to do that, we had no-one to talk to about culture. But we did have tender loving care from our parents, and we accepted what they said, so we never rebelled or said why we weren't allowed.

I don't know if boys are allowed more freedom, they are very demanding, aren't they? They always want more, because I have a brother, I grew up with a brother, and he's only three years younger than me. Whatever he wanted, he got. I didn't even want the same as him, the same things - he wanted to be out, he wanted to go with his friends, at the age of 18 he'd help my dad in his business to get pocket money as well, but he had money to spend as well, so he'd go out with his friends. He wanted a car, so he had to pass his driving test, he got a car.

When my mum came, she always wore a sari, and you know what a sari is - six metres, four yards of fabric. She used to buy fabric from Lewis's and places like that, and she didn't go without a sari. Like salwar kameezes, they weren't around when we were growing up, we'd wear trousers and tops, and some people would wear dresses on top of trousers just to get the effect of Shalwar Kameez.

I don't think my parents would even know who I went to school with, they wouldn't know their names, they wouldn't know where that person lived, but when you're Asian, they tend to sort of know. But with other people, they can't seem to keep track, 'cos they don't mix in the same circles. So everything else is sort of too dangerous to even imagine. But we didn't go out. Like, my daughter, she goes out with her groups of friends very rarely, but she'll tell me, "Why can't I go to some places where my friends are going?"

Women and the Community: Ananna House

Ananna have advice drop-in sessions and we advise on different issues like housing, DSS, immigration, education - all sorts of advice. And we have different activities as well. We have two English classes in a week, three sewing and dressmaking classes, one keep fit and healthy living class, one session of mother and toddler group. Other than that, we have a health project and mental health project. We work with the Bangladeshi women on mental health and health issues, and we have a young girls' worker as well, who works with young girls.

We have built up a good network with other voluntary organisations, and other statutory organisations. We work quite closely with health visitors, and CPN, and also we've built up contact with other voluntary organisations, the City Council as well, where we could refer women to go there for different service provisions which we can't provide here.

The project has developed a lot; we started with three part-time posts, and we have 7 part-time posts now, and three session crèche workers. We have about 15 volunteers because the Bangladeshi community is constantly growing in central Manchester. A lot of Bangladeshi families are coming out from other cities like Birmingham or London, because they have some relatives here. And also, some of the men are bringing their wives and families now, and some are getting married and bringing their wives or husbands here. So it's constantly growing, so the needs are constantly growing as well, and we can't fulfil all the needs without more staff, more funding, more volunteers.

The needs of Women in Manchester's Bangladeshi Community

Twelve years back, I don't think I had clear understanding about Bangladeshi women's needs. But because I have been working closely with the community for such a long time I understand their needs more and I am more committed to meeting their needs. We have seen changes in some women and their family as well, which is very rewarding. But we should do more, and continue to do what we're doing to benefit more women.

I was one of the sisters in the Bangladeshi community in Manchester who saw the need for a women's organisation. We have done a lot of hard work visiting the community and we have a whole lot of events and functions, seasonally everywhere. And we have done a lot of positive things to give back to the community. We have put in a lot of hard work to make it a success. We have a gained a lot of respect and I have gained a lot of interests and a lot of benefits through this.

The most important thing is that this is an English-speaking country, so I think women need to learn English. Any woman coming to this country for the first time from any culture should go to an ESOL class. They must also know the health issues of this country. They must know the health centres and the health workers, through which they can have a lot of benefits for their own families and their friends and other people.

I think it is very important that the community is represented, but at the same time I think it's also very important that people represent themselves as well. Everyone should feel that they have a role to play in society – they should not just rely on organisations to represent their views and their thoughts and their opinions. Sometimes, organisations are not connected to what's going on and how people feel at a grass roots level.

I feel that it's very important that everyone should know how to access decision making, how to influence change, and to make sure that they can play an active part in their community, whatever that is. So even as a mother who doesn't speak English, she should be able to play an active part in the mother and toddler group. Or as a student you should be able to play an active part in your neighbourhood, in terms of what happens around you, around policing or around leisure facilities or play areas – they should all have an opportunity to do that.

A woman has to learn about this culture, not see things negatively. I have come from another country so my views are different, but I'm liking it here now - it's my second home.

People who come from developing countries, they come with imagination. The women come with a lot of imagination, a lot of money, a lot of good food, and a lot of jobs. But in reality, this country is different, so I'd suggest that any woman coming to this country, they must know different organisations, different activity centres, etc. to achieve betterment in their lives. There are Women's Projects, Men's Projects and Family Projects. All these centres provide for their benefit: for computer learning, sewing, there are crèche facilities, etc., and other facilities, like seasonal activities for their children, themselves, etc. It is better if they can go to a place where those people can educate them for a better life and enjoy the country, enjoy their stay in this country. Because mostly people who come from our countries come to stay here, and it may not be that good at the beginning, but the ending must be good. That's what I expect and pray for them.

The Banner

The banner shown on the back cover was designed by the young people from Burnage High School for Boys and Levenshulme High School for Girls.

The images chosen represent the pioneering and rich cultural spirit of Bangladesh and its links with Manchester through trade and settlement. They depict significant buildings such as the War Memorial in Dhaka, while the Mills symbolise the textile industry in Manchester. Also chosen were symbols of both Bangladesh and Manchester: the Royal Bengal Tiger, the national animal of Bangladesh; the iconic flowers: the Water-lily of Bangladesh and the Red Rose of Manchester, and Lancashire; and Waterways - to represent the rivers and canals of Bangladesh and Manchester.

Key political and cultural figures also feature: Rabindranath Tagore (artist and poet), L.S.Lowry, (artist) Begum Rokeya (Founder of the Movement for Womens' Rights and Muslim Girls Education), Emmeline Pankhurst (suffragette),Sheikh Mujibur Rahman,(Liberator of Bangladesh).

The banner was made using Jute, which was, until recently, the chief export of Bangladesh. The banner was made at the People's History Museum, Manchester.

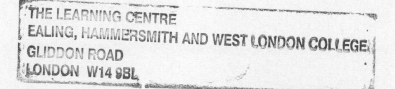